To

From

the essential
TAROT

BY ROSALIND SIMMONS

PETER PAUPER PRESS, INC.
Rye Brook, New York

Many thanks to Virginia Reynolds for her advice and assistance.

Illustrations copyright © 2002 Mary Hanson-Roberts
Hanson-Roberts Tarot Deck © 1985
by U.S. Games Systems, Inc., Stamford, CT.
Further reproduction prohibited.

Designed by Heather Zschock

the essential
TAROT

Contents

What does tomorrow hold for us?

*P*eople throughout the ages have had a fascination with predicting the future. The Tarot is an ancient method used to divine the future using cards inscribed with mysterious symbols and images. Scholars think that the Tarot originated over 3,000 years ago in the Middle East. "Tarot" may derive from the Kabbalistic word "Torah"—the sacred text of Judaism. Tarot cards and fortune telling became popular in Europe in the fourteenth century.

Many strands of esoteric lore are woven into the images of the Tarot, including Egyptian religious ideas, astrological symbols, and the iconography of Freemasonry. Modern Tarot cards range from the traditional to the avant garde.

The Tarot deck is made up of 78 cards divided into two categories, the Major and Minor Arcana. The 22 cards in the Major Arcana represent the forces

0 La Fou   0 II Matto
0 The Fool
0 Der Narr   0 El Loco

that influence our lives as well as the lessons life teaches us. The Minor Arcana, divided into four suits, are the forerunners of modern-day playing cards.

Before beginning your mystical journey through the Tarot, divide the cards into Major and Minor Arcana. Handle the deck often. As the images become familiar, your psychic energy will penetrate the cards. Once you have established a connection with your Tarot, wrap it in a piece of silk and keep it in a pouch or box when not in use, preferably in the east corner of your home.

♠ ♥ ♦ ♣

How to Give a Reading

Try to conduct your Tarot readings in a tranquil space. Noise and distractions interrupt the energy flow and can result in a fragmented reading. The Reader and the Questioner—the person whose cards are to be read—should clear their minds of extraneous thoughts and concentrate on the cards. Use a table and two chairs for the reading.

Before beginning, it is essential that you recognize the effect that you may have upon the Questioner. The most ancient rule applies here: first, do no harm. Use caution at all times. Whenever possible, steer the Questioner in a positive direction. Keep things upbeat.

Although you handle the cards carefully and maintain a focused attitude, a

Tarot reading should be fun for both Reader and Questioner. Your job is to help the Questioner take constructive action to realize important goals and make

positive life changes.

At the beginning of the reading, the Questioner formulates a specific question, and then focuses on that question while shuffling the cards. The Questioner now states the question aloud to the Reader while continuing to shuffle the deck face down. By handling the cards, the Questioner imbues them with personal magnetism, creating a rapport between the subconscious and the cards.

After the Questioner hands the face-down deck to the Reader, the Reader lays the cards out in formation (see pages 15 and 20-21). Always read the cards from the Reader's position, following the sequence indicated for the spread.

Turn the cards over from left to right so that they point in the same direction as when placed on the table by the Questioner. The cards facing the Reader—"upright"—indicate a strong positive reading. The cards facing the Questioner—"reversed" or "inverted"—can have a weaker meaning, or the opposite meaning of the upright card.

The majority of the cards when turned over should be in the upright position. If the first card you turn over is upside down, the Questioner may have mistakenly handed you the deck upside down. Turn all cards over from bottom to top to reverse their direction. In any reading, if more than half the cards are reversed, you may also reverse each card, so that more than half the cards will appear upright.

Remember, every reading is different. It is important to note subtle cues from the Questioner. A Questioner concerned with health matters will benefit less from a romantic interpretation of the cards. Sometimes you can reveal unconscious issues and help open the door to spiritual growth in unexpected ways. Let your intuition be your guide.

♠ ♥ ♦ ♣

The Ten Card Spread, or Celtic Cross

This spread is one of the most popular and effective ways of using the Tarot for predictions. The Reader lays out ten cards according to the diagram, then turns over the first six cards one at a time, placing them face up. Begin the reading in the following order:

CARD 1: PRESENT POSITION

This represents the immediate circumstances in which the Questioner currently lives. It shows influences at work right

The Ten Card Spread, or Celtic Cross

now. It also represents the Questioner.

CARD 2: IMMEDIATE INFLUENCES

This card illustrates obstacles that the Questioner faces, or influences lying just ahead. We say that this card *crosses* the Questioner.

CARD 3: GOAL OR DESTINY

Represents the Questioner's goal, and indicates what the Questioner can expect given the current state of affairs. It can also give a clue to the Questioner's hopes and fears about the future. This card *crowns* the Questioner.

CARD 4: DISTANT PAST FOUNDATION

Explains how the current situation came about, based on broad events that have already taken place. It can include the Questioner's personal history or other background information, including childhood or early life experiences. This card is *behind* the Questioner.

CARD 5: RECENT PAST EVENTS

Indicates events in the recent past and actions or behavior in the distant past that influence the current situation or form the underpinning of present attitudes. This card is *beneath* the Questioner.

CARD 6: FUTURE INFLUENCE

This card presents influences in the near future, including other people entering the picture and short-term changes that may occur.

After the first six cards have been interpreted, the Reader should turn over the remaining cards. Place them in a vertical line to the right of the first six, working from bottom to top (see p. 15).

CARD 7: ABOUT THE QUESTIONER

This card indicates how the Questioner feels about the present situation. It may reveal a course of action, as well as suggest the role that the Questioner must play in directing future events.

CARD 8: ENVIRONMENTAL FACTORS

Represents people and outside factors that may affect the outcome. This card can also point to the Questioner's relationship to other people. How much control can the Questioner exert over the eventual resolution of the situation?

CARD 9: INNER EMOTIONS

What fears trouble the Questioner? What does the Questioner secretly wish for? This card divulges the hidden desires and attitudes of the Questioner, as well as upcoming changes in the Questioner's perspective.

CARD 10: FINAL RESULT

This card reveals the ultimate outcome of the situation if events continue in their present course, based on the influences described by the other cards in the spread.

The Seven Card or

If the Questioner
has a specific problem or
obstacle to overcome, this is a
good spread for obtaining a quick
answer. The Questioner should shuffle
the cards and hand them to the Reader,
who will lay them out according to the

Horseshoe Spread

diagram. They are
interpreted from left to
right, as follows: 1. The Past;
2. The Present; 3. What Is Helping;
4. Obstacles to Overcome; 5. Attitudes of
Others; 6. What the Questioner Should
Do; 7. The Outcome.

THE MAJOR ARCANA

♠ ♥ ♦ ♣

The cards of the Major Arcana
offer us the broad categories of
the stages and lessons of life: love,
change, spirituality, morality. . .
They are the "big guns" of the
Tarot, almost larger than life.
Beginning with The Fool (0) and
ending with The World (XXI),
they form a complete allegory
depicting the circle of life.

0 The Fool

Ruled by Uranus, the powerful and unpredictable Roman sky god. This card portrays a young, carefree traveler embarking on life's journey. The bag on his shoulder holds the tools of life, and the white rose denotes pure intentions. Indicates a willingness to leap into the unknown and start anew.

REVERSED: Energy is at a low ebb. You are unable to make a balanced decision or to move forward.

I The Magician

Ruled by Mercury, the messenger of the gods. A strong man lifts a wand, while the tools of magical practice are set before him. Signifies the channeling of life force from above to below. This deeply masculine card suggests powerful energy. The Magician has the ability to summon new ideas.

REVERSED: Could indicate deception or the need to be careful where you put your trust.

II High Priestess

Ruled by the Moon. With the mark of Isis on her forehead and a crucifix around her neck—symbols of spirituality—she is balanced between the pillars of peace and severity. Signifies a mystical quietness; something remains hidden, so do not rush. Remain in a state of balance. With patience and intuition, all will be revealed.

REVERSED: Suggests vanity, instability, selfishness, deception.

III The Empress

Ruled by Venus, the Roman goddess of
love. Symbolizes the power of mother-
hood, the earth, and practical wisdom.
With a garland of stars and images of
fruits, the Empress is both
beautiful and bountiful. The stars
in her crown represent the signs of the
Zodiac, indicating that she is the mother
of all. This card suggests luxury and
abundance, and could indicate
pregnancy.

REVERSED: Overindulgence;
enjoyment of sensual pleasure; a tendency
to become domineering; barrenness.

IV The Emperor

Associated with the sign of Aries, the ram, the Emperor represents the earthly father. Depicted as the enthroned Roman emperor, he is the personification of temporal power. Suggests the accumulation of material wealth. Although disciplined and visionary, he keeps his emotions under wraps. Can also indicate a desire for independence.

REVERSED: Signifies rigidity; lack of self-control; an immature approach to life; a miserly nature.

V The Hierophant

Associated with the sign of Taurus, the bull. With a scepter in one hand and the other raised in blessing, he symbolizes the pope, the spiritual father, and the trinity—mind, body, spirit. He also represents organized religion or orthodox ideas. The card offers mercy and compassion and indicates a need for approval and conformity.

V Le Pape   V Il Papa
V The Hierophant
V Der Hohepriester   V El Papa

REVERSED: You are often unconventional and show a disregard for the rules.

VI The Lovers

Associated with the sign of Gemini, the twins. The image depicts lovers in an embrace, while an angel looks on. Gemini seeks a soul mate, a new love. This card suggests love, friendship, and partnership. Also represents the duality of earthly and divine love.

REVERSED: Quarrels can lead to separation. Infidelity can lead to marital difficulties. Be careful not to make hasty or unwise choices.

VII The Chariot

Linked to Cancer and the Moon. Twin sphinxes—one black, one white—draw a chariot emblazoned with the symbol of yin and yang. Balance negative and positive forces to achieve success. Maintain focus

and attend to details. You may be going on a long journey...

REVERSED: Denotes a lack of control; reverting to bad habits; a failure to follow through. Also possible setbacks with travel arrangements.

VII Le Chariot   VII Il Carro
VII The Chariot
VII Der Triumphwagen   VII El Carro

VIII Strength

Linked to the sign of Leo. The lion is a sexual animal, but his base instincts are checked by the caress of a maiden.

Message: Use your head and not your heart. Exercise restraint; hold your power in reserve. Courage and fortitude will bring success. Could signify healing qualities.

REVERSED: Indicates weakness and lack of self-control. Also symbolizes a lack of confidence, or even cowardice.

IX The Hermit

Associated with the sign of Virgo, the natural healer of the Zodiac. An old man leaning on a staff holds up a shining lantern. He shows the way to wisdom and enlightenment. This strong healing card suggests looking inward, seeking the inner path; an opportunity for self-knowledge.

REVERSED: Can represent loneliness and depression; impetuosity. Beware of hasty decisions.

X Wheel of Fortune

Ruled by Jupiter, the planet of expansion. This card can indicate a turn for the better, or receiving one's just reward for past deeds. Fortune, power, movement, and change are all here.

The wheel turns, revealing the cyclical nature of life.

REVERSED: Fickle fate; a turn for the worse. Blind optimism can lead to failure.

XI Justice

Associated with the sign of Libra, the scales. Justice holds a sword in one hand and the scales in the other. Decisions will be made—fairly. Suggests a possible court appearance. Can relate to wills or divorce.

REVERSED: Indicates prejudice or unreasonable decisions, legal or otherwise. Pay attention to what people are saying—they may not be completely forthright.

XII The Hanged Man

Calm and alert, the Hanged Man doesn't appear uncomfortable in his suspended state. Suggests a step backward, a distancing from everyday concerns. Indicates a period of rest and reassessment. Something new is on the horizon, but you must be patient.

REVERSED:

Unwillingness to make sacrifices; sacrifices made for the wrong reasons. Effort is required before the situation improves.

XIII Death

A skeletal rider on a pale horse bears the banner of a white rose. This card usually indicates rebirth or transition rather than physical death. Accept change so that rebirth can occur. Let go of past issues holding you back.

XIII La Mort   XIII La Morte
XIII Death
XIII Der Tod   XIII La Muerte

REVERSED: Someone refuses to budge, even for his or her own good. Possible loss of a friendship. Beware of accidents.

XIV Temperance

Linked with the sign of Sagittarius, the archer. An angel pours liquid from one vessel into another, blending the essences. This card represents a mixing of elements within oneself and within relationships. Reach into the past for continuity that you can carry into the future. This auspicious card brings good health.

REVERSED:

Disharmony; frustration. People are working at cross-purposes.

XV The Devil

Associated with Capricorn, the goat. A tethered couple looks away in misery under the Devil's yoke. Represents emotional, spiritual, physical bondage; ficial attachments or relationships based on

material gain. These chains can be broken with willpower. Can also relate to deviant sexual tendencies or cults.

REVERSED: You face bad habits or addictions. Take heart—these afflictions can be overcome.

XVI The Tower

Ruled by Mars, the Roman god of war. Lightning strikes the Tower, and its golden crown crashes earthward. Outmoded structures are smashed cleanly, leaving the way open to complete change. The Tower is a card of radical transformation. A partnership may suddenly dissolve. Check the structure of your home!

REVERSED: Trapped by old habits? It may be time to dig out of your rut.

XVII The Star

Coupled with the sign of Aquarius. Just as the young woman pours water, Aquarius pours forth creativity and new ideas. This card denotes hope and inspiration, perhaps from an unexpected source. The foundation is sound; change is natural and balanced. A bright future is in store.

REVERSED: You may face disappointment, perhaps due to your own stubbornness. An unfulfilling social or business association is coming to an end. Good riddance!

XVIII The Moon

The Moon rules the subconscious. Psychic powers are revealed; intuition is strong. As the Moon waxes and wanes, beware of deception and the shifting sands of superficial relationships. Also suggests that unusual, supernatural events may occur. A touch of lunacy is in the air.

REVERSED: Deceptions are unmasked. Small mistakes can be corrected.

XIX The Sun

A cherub rides a white pony through a field of sunflowers under a benevolent sun. Solar energy is powerful and fulfilling, bringing growth, contentment, and positive energy. Happy relationships and satisfying creative endeavors follow. Could be the time to expand your horizons, professionally or socially.

REVERSED: Could indicate blocked energy or setbacks. Keep an eye on important relationships.

XX Judgment

Ruled by Pluto, the god of the underworld. An angel sounds a trumpet, suggestive of the final judgment. This is a card of transformation. A fresh start is possible. It is time to forgive and forget, or perhaps do some soul-searching. A promotion may be in the works.

REVERSED: Stop delaying the inevitable. Indecision can lead to missed opportunities.

XXI The World

A robed figure commands the elements and forces of the universe. This card represents the completion of life's circle and mystical unity with the cosmos. The power of transcendence is within reach.

can attain worldly success and liberation through spiritual rebirth.

REVERSED: Success may be delayed. You are not quite there yet. Time to filter out imperfections and refine your vision.

49

THE MINOR ARCANA

♠ ♥ ♦ ♣

The Minor Arcana consist
of four suits of 14 cards each,
totaling 56 cards. They
represent many of life's
everyday situations—material
concerns, relationships,
nitty-gritty details. The
Court cards often represent
the people in our lives.

The Court Cards

KINGS: Represent older, powerful married men (fathers) or young men mature for their years; men of knowledge and wisdom.

QUEENS: Mother figures and adult women.

KNIGHTS: Young men who are usually single; older men who are young at heart or exceptionally dynamic.

PAGES: Represent beginnings—young, unmarried people; novices, inexperienced individuals. Pages are messengers.

THE SUIT OF PENTACLES

(DIAMONDS)

The Pentacle is a type of medieval coin,
depicted with a five-pointed star,
or pentagram. The Pentacles concern
our physical selves—all things connected
with the element of earth: property,
work, finances, practical matters. They
are associated with the earth signs of the
Zodiac: Taurus, Virgo, and Capricorn.

◆

The physical characteristics of Pentacles
and people represented by this suit
include dark hair and eyes, dark or olive
complexions, and a sturdy build.

King of Pentacles

Dressed in rich robes, the King is surrounded by the trappings of success—castle,
vineyards, cattle. He's a man at the
top of his game—tough, but an
excellent manager, and a devoted
husband and
friend. Could suggest
agricultural pursuits—or
stock market holdings.

REVERSED: A ruthless
person with little regard
for morality. This King
squanders his largesse.

Queen of Pentacles

Surrounded by fruit and flowers, the dark-haired Queen holds a rabbit—familiar symbol of fertility. Sensual and earthy, she enjoys abundance in many areas of her life. A lover of luxury, she is quick to share her wealth.

REVERSED: This Queen neglects her responsibilities, keeping up appearances regardless of circumstances.

Knight of Pentacles

The Knight is depicted in carefully tilled, rolling fields—the country squire on his estate. He takes his responsibilities seriously, and finishes what he starts. Loves the natural world.

REVERSED: Lacks imagination and follow-through; content to let things slide.

Page of Pentacles

The Page is lost in thought, focused on
the coin before him. This is the card
of the scholar. The Page has a thirst for
knowledge and pursues it diligently.
REVERSED: Disordered, illogical,
or rebellious thinking.

X Pentacles

An old man surrounded by family and possessions contentedly strokes a dog. Life is full. Wealth will be passed down through the generations. The family is safe and secure.

Dix des Deniers   Dieci di Denari
Ten of Pentacles
Zehn-Münzen   Diez de Oros

REVERSED: Loss of inheritance or position through dissipation or gambling. Don't take risks now—the odds are against you.

IX Pentacles

A woman stands in a vineyard holding a rare bird. Wisdom, knowledge, and talent are present, but no love life; this is a lonely time, to be met with a measure of detachment. Success, recognition, and wealth will follow.

Neuf des Deniers · Nove di Denari
Nine of Pentacles
Neun-Münzen · Nueve de Oros

REVERSED: Take extra care of your treasures—both friendships and material possessions. It's a good time to insure that priceless vase.

VIII Pentacles

A young craftsman, his tools around him, carefully examines his handiwork. You're a quick study. Advance your craft with conscientious effort. Success can be achieved through old-fashioned hard work.

REVERSED: Lack of ambition; excessive materialism; failure.

VII Pentacles

A weary young peasant rests at the end of a long day in the field. You are working hard, but more consistent effort is needed.

This card is about patience. Things will happen, but not now.

Sept des Deniers · Sette di Denari
Seven of Pentacles
Sieben-Münzen · Siete de Oros

REVERSED:

Impatience could lead to risky investments.

VI Pentacles

As he measures his wealth, the rich man holds out some coins to the poor. This is the card of the philanthropist. Generosity will be rewarded and loans will be repaid.

REVERSED:

Bad debt, unpaid loans; selfish behavior.

V Pentacles

Cinq des Deniers · Cinque di Denari
Five of Pentacles
Fünf-Münzen · Cinco de Oros

Two beggars pass a church window, but fail to see the light within. Are you so focused on your own distress that you fail to see that aid is at hand? This card could indicate errors and missed opportunities leading to financial trouble. Help is available—don't be afraid to ask.

REVERSED: The worst has passed. Hard times can be overcome.

IV Pentacles

The miser clings to his goods with all his might. He can't move, because he's holding on with his feet. This card is a hint to loosen your grip on material things, in order to help restore the flow of creativity and energy.

REVERSED: Obstacles stand in the way of material gain. Expect delays.

III Pentacles

The sculptor is hard at work in a church building. This is the card of the master craftsman. Unlike the VIII of Pentacles—the Apprentice—this card indicates the pinnacle of one's profession. People look up to you and admire your good example.

REVERSED: Sloppy work or inattention to detail. You can do better!

Trois des Deniers — Tre di Denari
Three of Pentacles
Drei-Münzen — Tres de Oros

II Pentacles

A youth juggles on the beach, oblivious to the stormy seas. Juggling is a difficult skill to learn. Don't lose sight of other circumstances as you try to balance two areas of your life. Don't take on more than you can handle.

REVERSED: You appear skilled at multi-tasking—but are you putting on a false front? It's not as easy as it looks.

Deux de Deniers Due di Denari
Two of Pentacles
Zwei Münzen Dos de Oros

Ace of Pentacles

A large Pentacle in the sky rests upon a bed of lilies, surrounded by golden clouds. Aces signify largesse and new beginnings. Here come pennies from heaven! Anticipate a new career, sudden prosperity, opportunities for tremendous growth.

REVERSED: Wealth doesn't buy happiness. Careful: Are you squandering money needlessly? Look to the pennies.

THE SUIT OF CUPS

(HEARTS)

Cups are connected to emotions,
relationships, friendship, and romance.
They are also associated with the element
of water, and water signs of the Zodiac:
Cancer, Scorpio, and Pisces.

♥

People represented by this suit usually
have blonde or light brown hair, and blue
or green eyes. The suit can also refer to
people with an artistic temperament.

King of Cups

Roi des Coupes — Re di Coppe
King of Cups
Kelchs-König — Rey de Copas

Like Neptune, the King of Cups reigns over the sea. His authority calms turbulent waters. He is creative and compassionate—often a doctor or counselor.

REVERSED: Watch out! This man is slippery as a fish.

Queen of Cups

This queen drinks deeply from the cup of life. Her emotions and sexuality are intense; she relies on intuition before intellect.

REVERSED: Be wary of a self-indulgent or wayward morality.

Knight of Cups

Astride a white steed, this knight gazes upon a chalice—the Holy Grail?—as the road winds before him. This attractive and persuasive individual is on a quest, perhaps romantic or spiritual. An invitation or proposal is on the way.

REVERSED: This glib fellow should be viewed with suspicion. He is not what he appears to be.

Page of Cups

A fish emerges from the cup, to the Page's surprise. Unexpected news is on the way; with the fish, it is likely to be spiritual. The Page is sensitive, thoughtful, helpful, loyal.

REVERSED: This young person is easily influenced or distracted.

X Cups

A happy family beholds the rainbow in a scene of great joy. This card signifies fulfillment, happiness, and domestic harmony.

REVERSED: The family is squabbling over petty issues. Don't sweat the small stuff!

Dix des Coupes   Dieci di Coppe
Ten of Cups
Zehn-Kelche   Diez de Copas

IX Cups

Surrounded by golden cups, a man beams happily. The peacock feather in his hat denotes good luck. This "Wish Card" promises that a wish, probably of a material nature, will be granted to the Questioner.

REVERSED: Errors or obstacles stand in the way of success. Don't allow an excess of confidence to blind you to the truth.

Neuf des Coupes Nove di Coppe
Nine of Cups
Neun-Kelche Nueve de Copas

VIII Cups

A pilgrim flees into the night under the watchful gaze of the moon. Don't walk away from a situation just before its completion; don't turn your back on success. You may be leaving a long-standing relationship. . .

REVERSED: Projects are completed. You will reap the rewards of your diligence. Expect a party or festive event.

VII Cups

Conjured by a wizard, fantastic creations emerge from the cups. Stop building castles in the air. Don't be distracted by flights of fancy.

Sept des Coupes — Sette di Coppe
Seven of Cups
Sieben Kelche — Siete de Copas

REVERSED: Cut through the fluff and get to the heart of the matter. Your willpower will carry you forward.

VI Cups

In a peaceful country scene, children frolic among cups of flowers. People emerge from your past; you feel nostalgia for days gone by. You long for a lost love.

REVERSED: The future will arrive sooner than you think! Look to what lies ahead and prepare for a change.

V Cups

Although two of the cups are filled, the figure wearing the "cloak of mourning" sees only what has spilled. You feel remorse over a severed relationship or unfulfilled dream. "If only..."

REVERSED: A reunion is at hand. Perhaps an old friend will drop in. The outlook is hopeful.

IV Cups

As a youth contemplates three cups, a hand descends from a cloud to offer a fourth. You are jaded or bored with life. Perhaps a bad experience has caused you to withdraw. Are you traversing a period of stagnation?

REVERSED:

Re-emerging into the world. New possibilities and ideas abound. Perhaps you've adopted a "new look."

Quatre des Coupes Quattro di Coppe
Four of Cups
Vier-Kelche Cuatro de Copas

III Cups

The three maidens in the garden correspond to the three Graces. Surrounded by bowers of blooms, they raise their cups in celebration. It's party time! Relax and take credit for a job well done. You may be moving toward retirement. . .

REVERSED:

Overindulgence in pleasurable activities. Stop taking your good fortune for granted.

Trois des Coupes   Tre di Coppe
Three of Cups
Drei-Kelche   Tres de Copas

A young couple is absorbed only in each other. This is the card of passion and romance. Your relationship will enter a new and important phase. Will an engagement or marriage result? Intense eroticism.

REVERSED: A tumultuous relationship has too many ups and downs. Open the lines of communication to avoid misunderstandings.

Ace of Cups

Streams of life-giving water flow from the lovely chalice. Oh, bright beginnings! Is it the heady start of a love affair? You feel tremendous joy and optimism. Fertility, abundance.

REVERSED: Could be a false start, or an unfulfilling relationship. Take off the rose-colored glasses and see things as they are.

THE SUIT OF RODS

(CLUBS)

This is the suit of action and energy.
The Rods are always depicted sprouting
or flowering; they signify growth.
Also called Wands, Rods are associated
with the fire element and the fire
signs of the Zodiac: Aries, Leo,
and Sagittarius.

People with fair or red hair and
blue eyes make up the suit of Rods. They
often have freckles and athletic builds.

King of Rods

The King of Rods is depicted with the lion rampant at his back. He has the strength to back up his ideas and vision. This self-starter can rarely sit still. Honest and dependable; a natural leader and man of action.

REVERSED: Your extreme views prevent you from yielding to the opinions of others.

Queen of Rods

This lovely Queen has charms to soothe the savage beasts—witness the cat snoozing on her lap. The Sunshine Lady brings light and love to the people around her. This consummate hostess is also a tireless worker for charity.

REVERSED: You are jealous when crossed and fickle in your affections. You cannot be swayed.

Knight of Rods

The Knight bears the emblem of the dragon— fiery, passionate, and ready to take on the world. This is the sign of the explorer. Also signifies travel, adventure; a change of residence.

Cavalier des Bâtons   Cavaliere di Bastoni
Knight of Rods
Stäbe-Ritter   Caballo de Bastos

REVERSED: You lack focus and change course in mid-stream, often departing impetuously. You're quick to anger and tend to pick fights with people around you.

Page of Rods

Adorned with a medallion of the sun,
the Page is shouting out a message. Good
news is on the way. Don't be shy; make your
voice heard. **REVERSED:** Gossip is afoot.
Someone is telling tales about you.
Stop the rumors while you can.

X Rods

An old man is staggering
under the weight of
many burdens. Feeling
burnt out? The
pressure will ease
soon. Physical exercise
and relaxation will help
maintain your health.

Dix des Bâtons   Dieci di Bastoni
Ten of Rods
Zehn-Stäbe   Diez de Baston

REVERSED: Someone is working
against you. It's time to act—
before too much damage is done.

IX Rods

Already wounded, a worried man braces for the next salvo. This is the eye of the storm. The situation will worsen before it improves, but you are prepared.

REVERSED: Pay attention! Read the writing on the wall or you'll find misfortune. Beware of traps.

Neuf des Bâtons   Nove di Bastoni
Nine of Rods
Neun-Stäbe   Nueve de Bastos

VIII Rods

These rods fly through the air like javelins. The pace of change is speeding up. Don't be left behind. Could indicate an unexpected voyage.

REVERSED: If everyone goes off in different directions, nothing will be accomplished. Use teamwork.

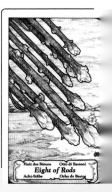

VII Rods

Sept des Bâtons   Sette di Bastoni
Seven of Rods
Sieben-Stäbe   Sept de Bâtons

A young man successfully wards off an attack with only a flowering rod. This is the card of the underdog. Despite overwhelming odds, victory is assured. Now is the time to take advantage of the situation. Carpe diem!

REVERSED: Doubt, uncertainty. Hesitation now could result in failure.

VI Rods

The laurel-bedecked hero returns victorious. Your hard work has paid off. Expect a bonus or reward. REVERSED: Could signify an empty victory, or someone else taking credit for your work.

V Rods

Are these youths playing—or fighting? Leadership is absent from this competition. If forces can be rallied, the struggle will prove fruitful. Suggests labor unions or political organizations.

Cinq des Bâtons   Cinque di Bastoni
Five of Rods
Fünf-Stäbe   Cinco de Bastos

REVERSED:
People won't cooperate. The situation is becoming more complicated. Decisions are difficult just now.

IV Rods

A lovely floral arch joins the flowering rods. This can signify the joining of two families in marriage. The

partnership will benefit everyone involved. Peace and harmony have been restored.

REVERSED: A flaw mars an otherwise perfect arrangement. The results fall short of expectations.

III Rods

Trois des Bâtons — Tre di Bastoni
Three of Rods
Drei-Stäbe — Tres de Bastos

A dignified man watches from the shore as ships return to the harbor. Trade and bargaining are on the horizon. Although compromise is necessary, you are negotiating from a position of strength.

REVERSED: Someone has a hidden agenda. Be sure offers of help are genuine. You hold the advantage, although you may not know it.

II Rods

He's got the whole world in his hands. It's all within reach. You're strong enough to change your dreams into reality. Be bold!

REVERSED: Try not to lose heart or let others hold you back. Keep the faith.

Ace of Rods

Everything is springing to life in this card. It can indicate virility or the birth of a child. Energy abounds. Could signify the beginning of an exciting new enterprise, career, or course of study.

REVERSED:

Although there's energy, the goal isn't defined and efforts are wasted. Don't be surprised if plans don't work out.

THE SUIT OF SWORDS
(SPADES)

Swords represent the more intellectual
side of life—situations where reason
prevails over emotions. Swords cut through
muddled thought and bring sudden clarity.
They are associated with the element
of air and the air signs of the Zodiac:
Gemini, Libra, and Aquarius.

♠

Swords usually indicate people with
brown hair and green, hazel, or brown
eyes. They also suggest people who
are good communicators.

King of Swords

The King of Swords is primed for action, his weapon ready, as he pauses to weigh the situation. He is highly analytical, often pursuing a career in law or publishing. His leadership is unquestioned.

Roi des Épées   Re di Spade
King of Swords
Schwerter-König   Rey de Espada

REVERSED: Stirring up controversy and discord; cruelty; mean-spiritedness.

Queen of Swords

The sword in the Queen's hand represents her quick wits—and her sharp tongue. The widow, like other women in difficulty, continues bravely despite loss. Her keen intelligence and cool, logical approach make her appear aloof.

REVERSED: This dangerous enemy can cut you to ribbons with her words. She who is normally rational now shows a closed mind.

Knight of Swords

Cavalier des Épées   Cavaliere di Spade
Knight of Swords
Schwerter-Ritter   Caballo de Espadas

The Knight charges bravely into battle. It's Sir Lancelot, defender of chivalry. He's a skilled warrior who rushes into situations without weighing the consequences. His charming nature gets him out of scrapes.

REVERSED: Because he falls in love at first sight, this man can choose the wrong woman. He is blind to his shortcomings.

Page of Swords

This perceptive young person is ready for action. The card signifies quick thinking. Can also indicate spying or trouble with the police.

REVERSED: Powers stronger than yours are at work. It's difficult to stay one step ahead of the situation. An impostor is found out.

X Swords

This is a card of perfect desolation. Major changes are on the way, and resistance is futile. A path clears itself, giving way to something new.

REVERSED:
Temporary improvement or gain. A quick profit but nothing lasting.

Losing sleep? Have the feeling that something's hanging over your head? This is the darkest hour before the dawn. Action is the antidote to worry.

REVERSED: Trust your intuition and suspicions about that certain person. Your doubts are well founded.

VIII Swords

A blindfolded and bound figure is surrounded by danger. This difficult situation cannot be ignored. If bad news comes, face it squarely, even if there is nothing you can do.

Huit des Epées   Otto di Spade
Eight of Swords
Acht-Schwerter   Ocho de Espadas

REVERSED: Past events come back to haunt you. A few extra safety precautions will prevent accidents.

VII Swords

A figure flees with five swords while leaving two behind. Your efforts will be partly successful. Perhaps it's time for a new plan. Don't let fantasies interfere with the task at hand.

REVERSED: Someone near to you is dispensing bad advice. Or— could you be the one who talks too much?

Sept des Épées   Sette di Spade
Seven of Swords
Sieben-Schwerter   Siete de Espadas

VI Swords

A strong man transports swords in a boat. Someone is going to cut you some slack—soon. Relief will come after a struggle. You may be taking a sea voyage.

REVERSED: An unexpected or unwelcome proposal. The situation cannot be resolved right now.

V Swords

Two unarmed figures take flight. Signifies a withdrawal after conflict, or a victory without peace. Be careful not to create a tense atmosphere. It's a bad time to make enemies.

REVERSED: An unsettled period in your life. A friend may need your support.

IV Swords

The knight reposes in his tomb. It's time to take a break from life's pressures. Can indicate someone in the hospital recovering from an illness; or a religious retreat.

Quatre des Epées   Quattro di Spade
Four of Swords
Vier Schwerter   Cuatro de Espadas

REVERSED: Proceed with caution. Progress will occur in small increments. You are searching for a lost object.

III Swords

Three swords in the heart warn of heart-break, adultery, and infidelity. You need to communicate with a loved one. Be sure to take care of health matters.

REVERSED:
Confusion and disor-der can lead to errors. Setting priorities will help ease your worries.

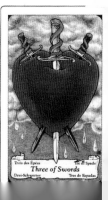

Trois des Épées   Tre di Spade
Three of Swords
Drei-Schwerter   Tres de Espadas

II Swords

The blindfold and crossed swords denote a situation that is delicately balanced. Diplomacy is required, but agreement can be reached.

Relations will warm up, but it will take time.

REVERSED:
Someone is not telling the whole story. A lie could upset the balance. Insist on complete honesty.

Ace of Swords

The sword and the wreath appear together. Order and just rule lead to abundance and prosperity. You are headed for success. You make an intellectual breakthrough, such as a discovery or the publication of a book.

REVERSED: The abuse of power can lead to discontent. Throwing up obstacles in another's path will only cause you embarrassment. Reexamine your motives.